All My Muses in One Room.

All My Muses in One Room

Ronald Acevedo

Contents

Dedications

To my queens Angela Vega, Maria Obando, and Gisselle "Ms. G" Gonzalez-Llano, this book is for you.

I'd like to begin with you, Mom. I want to say thank you for sacrificing all that you had to sacrifice in order to bring me into this world. I also want to thank you for bringing me into this amazing country, filled with so many wonderful opportunities. You always pushed me to be my very best, to believe in myself, and for that I cannot say thank you enough.
I hope I've made you and dad proud.

Sister, second mom, you showed me what it means to love, at such an early age. I thank you for that. It is because of you that I know what love should feel like. Thank you for loving me as your own, for protecting me always, and for always being my number #1 fan. I love you beyond words. You are my best friend. You have treated me like your other son and your baby brother. I hope I've made you proud.

Ms. Llano aka Ms. G, how do I begin this? I saved you for last because had it not been for you, I would've never written this book. The world should know who you are, and why it is I wrote this book. Teachers matter, and you matter so much to me.

Thank you for all that you do so selflessly, for the children, your students. You saved me from certain failure; not just in your class but also in life. The seventeen-year-old boy in me told you once that I wanted to quit, and so you kept me during lunch for a long time.

I complained for what I had perceived to be punishment, but time and wisdom would teach me otherwise. I despised reading literature, but I found a welcoming place writing poetry. As I live, I will never forget the day you stumbled upon one of my poems.

You found it hard to believe it was written by me, the boy who hated literature, but you had a plan. You asked me to read you my poems instead of the classroom literature. Then one day you spoke words into my life I never thought would come to fruition.

You said, "Young man, you're going to write a book one day." Well Ms. G, that day has come. You planted the seed. You watered it, and here now are the fruits of your labor. You have finally made a believer out of me.

Never again will I doubt myself. Thank you for everything you did for that seventeen-year-old boy. Thank you for what you did for this man. I love you.

Acknowledgements

It is impossible for me to name everyone who has inspired and encouraged me on this journey. I will begin by saying this, wow! I'm in so much disbelief that this moment has arrived. To the people who don't know me that will buy this book and share it with their friends, lovers and family. I hope this book can bring you some sort of happiness, that you are not alone, that you are heard and understood. I too have gone through those things you're so afraid to talk about. I hope this book can help you be kinder to yourself and all the things we experience in this journey called life. To the people in this city and all around that read my poems on social media or even come see me at my shows, thank you. It is because of you that I even have the courage to do this. To the ones that pushed me from early on, the ones that believed in me even when I didn't believe in myself, to the ones that told me to keep going, to keep pushing. Thank you.

I thank the following people from the deepest part of my soul. My amazing father, Freddy Acevedo, I will love you forever. Dad, you almost passed away on me, but you came back to life when I arrived in Nicaragua. God makes no mistakes. Thank you for coming back into my life. Thank you for showing me the amazing family I left behind. I hope to make you proud. To my brothers and sisters in my lovely country of Nicaragua: Ricardo, Javier, Carlos, Kevin, Freddy, Linda, Maritza, Luis, Rito, Julytza and Coralia. To my siblings here in Miami, Ismael, Alexandra, Alex, Felix, and Rosa. Thank you! Thank you to my friends, Oswaldo, William, Erickson, Matt, Rob, Stephanie , Jacks, Camila, Geo, Andres, Jeff, Steph, Sara, Erika, Ariel,

Andrea, Leticia, Phil, Derick G, Greg , Jas, Kim, Rob Lee, Jose, Eddie, Mike Bell, Carlos, Rocs, Vero, Jorge, Mike, Josh, Cherie, Marlon and Gigi, thank you all.

To Ms. Valdes and Mr. Brown, thank you from the bottom of my heart. Without you two this wouldn't have been possible. Thank you for believing in my vision. I love you both, May God keep blessing you always.

To my muses, you know who you are. Thank you for all the inspiration, for all the love and for giving me this passion.

This book is for you. I love you.

Foreword

The poet is an adept enchanter. His magic, words. Simply find your way downstream of the place he bares his soul and he will spellbind you without laying a single finger in your direction. At times he's like a skilled physician suturing wounds you've left unattended. Although, as surely as he can heal you, unquestionably, he can break the seal of wounds you thought long had been mended.

Permit him, and he will reflect your pains, passions, and demons like unperturbed water pooled in the deep of your silence. Immerse yourself in his words, and he'll reveal the bitter truth concealed between the saccharine lies you keep feeding yourself.

As I journeyed through my own room, revisiting mine own muses, I could not fight the urge to go back to a time and a place I wrestled with a demon I thought had long been exorcised.

> *"Yesterday was filled with anger and lots of desires. I'm a mixture of emotions and burning fire. It's a love hate thing that we both feel within."*

And with this I say, how unfortunate the one who's never ridden the ebbs and flows of a love that could not make up its mind. This is what I love most about poetry, its ability to transport you to places you've been, and places you haven't been. And who among us have not been to this place, caught in a tug-of-war between loving, and not wanting to love, though you know it is the very air that you need live?

And yet, this collection is not confined by the sentiments of romantic relationships. Take, for example, She Rocks a Scarf to Hide Those Scars. A chilling depiction of a demon too many of us have battled with either directly, or indirectly, domestic violence.

To be quite frank, All My Muses in One Room is just an honest piece of art. Ronald is truly unfiltered. One cannot help but be caught up in the strong undercurrent of love and love lost that runs throughout this collection. It is a difficult thing, being honest with one's self. It takes courage, and even a greater amount of courage to allow the world to flip through your soul the way the reader will flip through this poet's soul.

The reader should not be surprised to have a sense of uneasiness reading these words. He, or she might feel as though this poet had a court-side seat in their lives, because these poems will speak directly to them.

It has truly been an honor to read these words, if for nothing else, because I was transported to bitter times and to sweeter times. It is funny how we often think our stories are unique to us, that the paths we've traveled became overgrown once we passed on, but this collection of poems will show otherwise. For me, it was quite evident that Ronald and I have walked very similar paths. It was refreshing to see something so familiar from another perspective.

C.L. Brown, Author/Poet

Liquor Times.

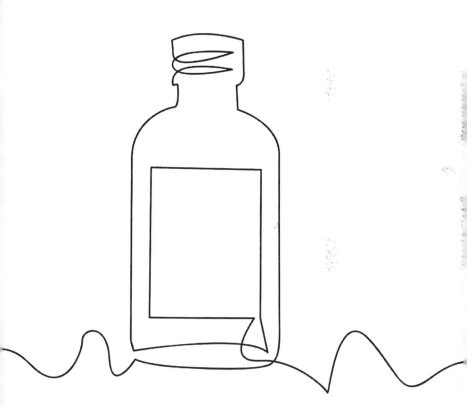

All My Muses in One Room

LIQUOR TIMES

I'm starting to miss my liquor time
I'm not an alcoholic but I pour this truth through
every liquor line
Like when my cousin used to say "look, look that
chick is hella fine"
We used to snatch these spirits, picking up women
through our favorite lines
Now I'm stuck in a moment that I can't define
They say I shouldn't date you because, for some
reason, girl you're always unfaithful
Remember the flowers I sent to you? You never
said thank you

I never thought someone so great could be so
ungrateful
Love's supposed to be beautiful and feelings
mutual, but this right here is unusual
So, now you got me feeling neutral
I'm only 22
I shouldn't be into you
I'm losing my focus
You did that on purpose
I'm bout to just curse bitch
I hope you enjoy it

I'm high as a motherfucker I swear I can barely see
I be dammed if I ever let another woman
take the best of me, but my ex pops
in my head subconsciously
And honestly, I would never let her bother me,
except my emotions took shots of this liquor
arousing the lust in me
So, now I want to sex you
Fuck a condom, let me protect you
I know you're heartless, and I'll someday regret you
Until then, blame it on this alcohol cause the sober
man in me would never disrespect you
My emotions built me up like Legos but now you're
gone and I'm left to pick up the pieces
Writing this drunk poetry between blank pages
because you never got the memo
Is this what life becomes when you're doing you?
Empty bottles, late night text, somebody that
knows somebody that knows your ex, trash full of
latex and pretty women that deceive you with
respect?
I guess I'm ready for what's next

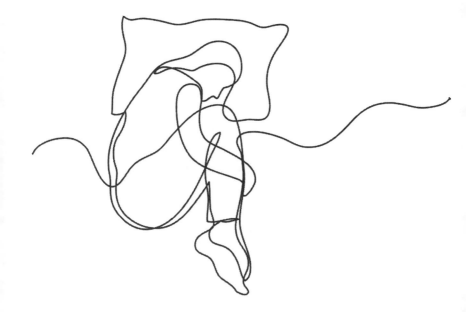

YOU HATE IT

You hate it when I lecture you, and tell you that I
told you so
Listing all the flaws of these men that you keep
going for
I guess your past has left you uncertain
Questioning yourself on why you do this
You're trying to change but moving on is the
hardest
And even though your goal is close,
it feels the farthest
Making the same mistakes, are you retarded?
Picking up men like waste management do garbage
Getting conversations that end before
they even get started
I see you've perfected letting your thoughts
sink in dark liquor
Hoping then you'll forget about him much quicker
I mean come on, you're not average, why allow him
to compare you?
I know the shit he does sometimes scares you
Letting shit fly out his mouth that
he can't ever take back
Slowly he's becoming your enemy
Now you're asking questions like, "Is this what
love's supposed to be?"
"Is this what God chose for me?"
That's the last time you'll pray for him cause you're
starting to have hate for him, and you hate it
Cause I told you so
It's time to let him know, that you have to let him
go

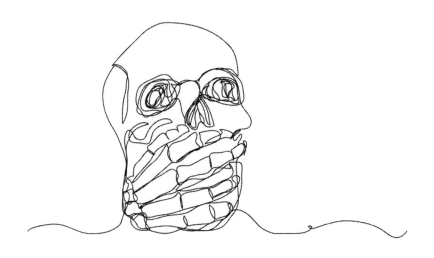

POISON

I am motivated
I am motivated by the thoughts of you
By the way you speak of me
By the way you express in bitterness who I am
I am motivated because you speak of me in a way I
will never speak of you
Unlike me, you have to fashion an idea of who I
am in order to hate me
You are so in denial about the feelings
I injected into you
You are full of anger
Full of hate
Full of poison

All My Muses in One Room

Your lips, as sweet as they look, suck the life out
of me when we kiss
Your eyes, as dark as they are, look upon me with
hatred and constant debate of how much you'd die
just to hate me
Your ears listen but only capture my greatest flaws
Your body, as sinful as can be, poisons me
every time I make love to you
You're worse than a loaded gun emptying
itself into my heart
You are the rose, full of thorns, ready to prick me
every time I get close

All My Muses in One Room

You are the douche bag, the one that I toast for
You are the "Runaway" girl Kanye West talks about
Vindictive and dominant, you're my addictive drug
You're as beautiful as the Devil was
as he fell from the sky
You are Eve, convincing me to bite from your
Apple You are the pure definition of the word sin
You are a virus that I can never kill
I am forever ill
I am filled with your poison
I am motivated

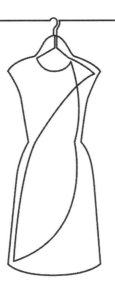

DEVIL IN A DRESS

You're the girl with the pretty lips and pretty eyes
telling me pretty lies
Let me ask you this, did you cheat?
And with who?
What's the name of the guy?
Looking down she replied, "I can't talk about it"
She just cried while I dried the tears from her eyes
She said, "I'm ungrateful. That is why I'm
unfaithful" "When we fight, I'm unable to control
my emotions" "I'm unstable"
"This is why I fought hard not to date you"
"I know, saying sorry does nothing for the pain
that I gave you"
"Baby, please don't blame yourself"
"I'm just a devil in a dress giving you hell"
That's all she said before leaving my heart to the
cold

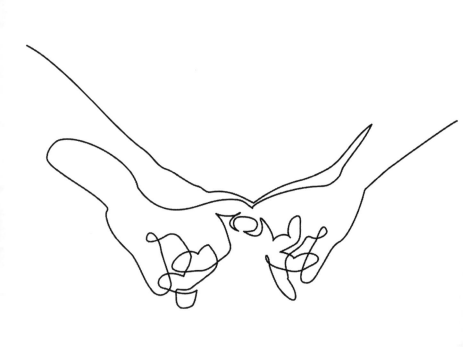

A DEDICATION (GOOD LOOKS)

To the daughters of the good mothers
The sisters of the good brothers
There will be none like you
This is beyond trying to wife you
You're the ones that a man has to pray for and
let God find you
You don't have to be reminded
because you already know
You're not trying to be out here all exposed
You know, like them other girls do?
Hoes!
You're greater than that
You don't like labels
You're a yes, or no type of girl
And if we're together, you're rocking with that
The rarest in my life, you're like an artifact
Something I may one day find, and if I lose it, I
will never get you back

LIFE'S A BITCH

You claim that you love me
That you miss me,
but you won't dare touch me,
or kiss me
Why must you disrespect me?
A nightmare is this?
Picture so clear it's vivid

That's what you told me
Words in your eye's screaming hold me,
adore me,
don't close the door,
please console me
You said, "baby how long do you think I'm going
to chase you?"
"You really do things sometimes that makes me
want to hate you"

"I'm with him, but he isn't you"
"He doesn't care like you do"
"He doesn't sex me like you do,
nor kiss it like you do,
nor hit it like you do"
"You got me addicted, committed"
"Now I'm all contradicted"
"How did we get to this?"
"You were my life, and I was your bitch"
"I guess it's true what they say,
life is a bitch"

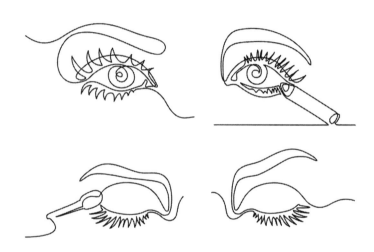

THE BREAK UP

And she said she wants to break up then make up
I was so upset, I said you ain't shit
without your makeup
Yea, you ain't shit without your makeup

YOU

I have no words to express how I feel for you, but
if love exists it lives inside of you
There's not a day that I do not think of you
I smile every time you cross my mind, but I hate it
because you're no longer mine and that's my fault
cause I let you go
That day I left my heart in the hospital because
ever since, every girl I've met has been an obstacle
and forgetting you has been impossible
So, I try to match your qualities to the next girl but
she will never be you
You, you're unique
You're one of a kind
You're special
You're everything I've hoped for and more
I really think that I will love you forever
Sincerely Ronald, my love letter

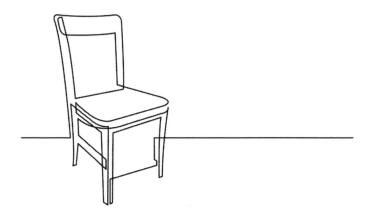

PRISON

It is safe to say that love is a prison, because I'm
trapped in you
I'll break any law to make you smile
To hear you laugh
I'll do time in the solitary confines of your mind,
sentencing you to happiness
If I could trap clouds in a jar, I would travel to the
highest mountain, the closest to heaven,
stealing pieces of rainbow-washed puffs of
perfection, just to let you know that you're
unrivaled
God must have molded luck when he decided to
make me, because nothing else explains why you're
the one holding me

All My Muses in One Room

Love is a prison, but no matter how trapped I am
inside of you, it isn't enough to keep us together
They say timing is everything, but when I'm inside
of you, time isn't anything
My mind lingers in the thoughts of you
See, you left and love closed its gates on me
All I do is sit around in this cell thinking about the
time I am serving because of you

All My Muses in One Room

See, this love has no parole
No judge
No witness
Just the memories of the laws I have broken to be
with you
So now I sit alone in this prison thinking of what
love can do to you
We were happy and free, but love has become the
prison you erected for me

PRISON PART II

I sit and I wonder
Why have I not learned?
I keep playing with fire expecting not to get burned
The feeling is ugly
I hate how I feel
Yearning for feelings one day I hope to kill
Your heart is frozen
In truth, it gives me chills
Sometimes I ask, is this even real?
Should love, this intense, feel so painful?
I guess this is how it's supposed to be
Love is a prison
Will I ever be free?

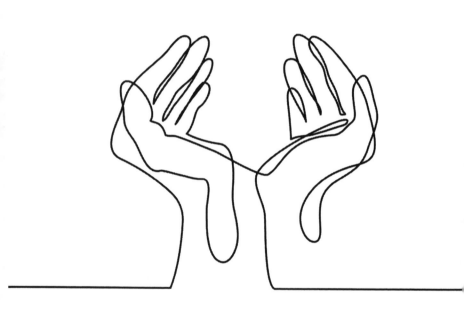

WHEN YOUR HEART TURNS COLD

You don't know how beautiful you were when your
lips did not lie,
your eyes did not cry,
and your face did not frown
When love meant something and hate meant
nothing So I must ask, what is it that you miss the
most?
The fact that I kept you close,
held you tight,
and told you that I'll always care the most?
I guess I waited too long, because your heart has
turned cold

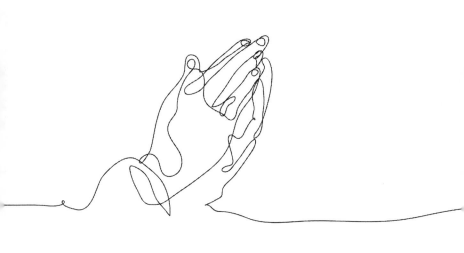

FOR ANGELA

I want to be the man my mother never had in her
life, because I want to love a woman like a man
should've loved my mother
I want to hold a woman like a man should've held
my mother
I want to be the father my father never was
I want to water my seeds not just plant them
I want to love
I want to love today,
tomorrow,
and forever

Dedicated to my mother

HOME IS WHERE THE HEART IS

They say home is where the heart is,
but what if you're homeless,
are you heartless?
I refuse to believe everything I see, because I once
saw love in her eyes as I watched her lying to me
I never thought this could happen
A man's faithfulness has never gifted a woman
blindness
Maybe it was his attractiveness
Maybe she never really saw me
Maybe I'm paranoid
You see, women who speak of fairytales get me
mad annoyed
How blind must you be to believe the illusions in
Disney movies?
All my life I was made to believe that love cures
everything as if love itself isn't a disease
Trust me, I've seen enough broken hearts
So I keep mine in a place far away from anyone
who would return it back to me void
Broken and almost destroyed
Home is where my heart is,
but what if your homeless,
are you then heartless?

LOVE HATE

Love hate, that is the great debate
This feeling inside I can't explain, because in every
moment we've shared we've felt pleasure and pain
Sometimes I wonder, why do you stay?
But then again, I ask myself the same question
every day
I remember when we met
Just a few hours, on our first date
I knew you would be hard to forget
Looking back at it, I can't help but smile
The things we've been through were wild
Are you tired?
Please don't answer
I'd rather not know, because I still can't let you go
The story of the lover I don't want to hate
Forever in my heart is not up for debate

MY NAME IS NOT PLAYER

Hi, my name is not player
But I know you see my cute little smirk and
seductive stares
I know that you think that all I want to do is see
you in your underwear
That the only thing I want from you is sex, but
take a moment to reflect and not neglect the point
that I am trying to get across
I carry this player badge like a cross and I'm nailed
to it by the sins you think I commit on the daily
But you're too late
You see, I've already sacrificed myself to this
liquor, thinking about all the women that hate me

Hi, my name is not player, and I hope that you
don't judge me by the women I keep in my
company
I am smart enough to know that my reputation told
you that I'm fucking one of them
I'll admit, I've failed the tests of temptation
I might even have a slight crush on one of them,
but you are not without sin, so don't you dare
allow that stone to leave your hands
I don't have to give you an explanation,
but maybe I genuinely like her

Hi, my name is not player, but I know for sure you
wear the badge of a hater
You're so closed minded
Your brain, you should go and find it
Instead of judging me,
harassing me,
and calling me names like "man whore",
"player",
"womanizer", same shit
If you took the time to get to know me
You'd have to admit that I'm much nicer
Much kinder

I'm more than just a boner
More than just lips spitting game to undress you
More than a snake taking you out to fancy places
with money that I don't have, just to impress you

Hi, my name is not player
So, the next time, before you set your lips to judge
me, please give your heart a chance
to get to know me

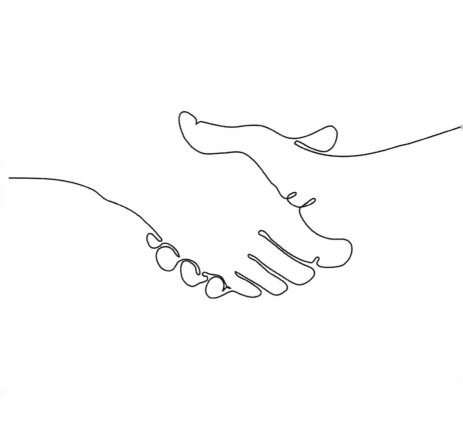

I ALWAYS HOLD ON LONGER

I always hold on longer
She might leave soon
She's the world to me
The stars and the moon
I kiss her softly
She might leave soon
The only thing that matters now is what we do
inside this room
I hope, to God, these words will come true
Because time is passing, and you might leave soon
If you never get to read this,
you'll never know how long I held on
I had so much more to write,
but you left so soon

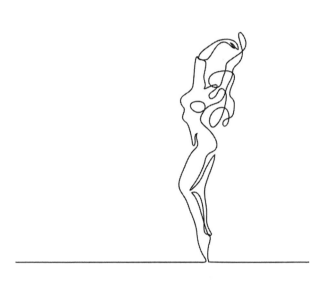

YOU TOO WILD

You too wild
You too fire
You this
You that
You over react
You say things you can't take back
You this
You that
You over react
You too wild
You too fire

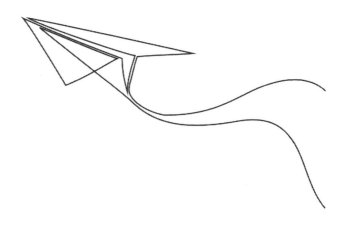

IS THIS PIECE ANOTHER MISTAKE?

Is this piece another mistake?
Should I roll it up,
throw it in the trash,
flip to a new page,
for a clean slate then start a remake?
I keep starting these relationships only to leave
them undone when I'm finished
Words unwritten because they wouldn't listen
They say creativity is allowing yourself to make
mistakes
Art is knowing which pieces to keep and which to
forsake
So here goes another shot
Another word forced upon this writer's block

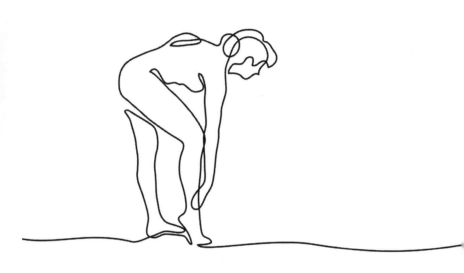

SHE ROCKS A SCARF TO HIDE THOSE SCARS

She rocks a scarf to hide those scars
She's ashamed of that man who beats her,
cheats her,
and mistreats her
She's afraid of pressing charges causes he's a
gangster and knows people
Five months pregnant,
but she cries every night in resentment,
regretting the day she met him
Hating herself
Falling into depression
Having no one to go to and no form of expression
Until that one night in the master bedroom
by the night table
She saw condom wrappers on the floor
by the TV cable

Now, for certain she knows he's unfaithful
Screaming her lungs out "why are you so
ungrateful?'
I'm seven months into pregnancy with your baby
boy, does this not bring you any joy?
So angry he became, grabbing her by the neck
She's trying to scream for help,
getting choked up by the pain
She's slowly losing consciousness trying to explain
"Baby, baby, what about our baby?"
"What about our baby?"
"Baby, baby, don't forget that I'm your lady"
Gasping for air, she slowly passed away
Her water broke
Now little baby's on the way
But his father fled the scene, and all the neighbors
heard was little baby's terrifying screams
Tell me who you love, and I'll tell you who you are
Baby Derick made it through his mother's pain and
scars

I wonder if he will ever know who his parents are
and what truly happened here and why they are
apart
The light always comes after the dark,
but why must we hurt those we love
Just because we refuse to see who we are
If he hit you once and you let him slide don't you
dare complain about them times you'll have to run
and hide
I don't mean to scare you
But when you choose to love someone, make sure
the feeling is mutual
Mental illness is real and so is domestic violence
So if you see something wrong please don't stay in
silence
The story of those scars under her scarf

HARD TIMES

I know times are hard and it's dark, but look at the
sky and see the stars
 There's a purpose of them being what they are as
there is one for you

SHE'S HAVING FITS AGAIN

She's having fits again like if she was a fucking kid
again
Don't you fucking kid again
Cause sometimes you treat me like your girl and
then like your bitch again
Screaming at me saying, "I called you ni**a,
but I bet you was with that other bitch I figured"
"How I'm pose' to feel?"
"How I'm pose' to act?"
"When you're with her, how I'm pose' to react?"
Cause when I call there you go always canceling

There she goes having fits again,
and then she said if she had kids,
I'd be the only reason why
she would never have kids again!
And that's when I called her a bitch again
You want to jump and kick again?
You want to fight and have fits again?

All My Muses in One Room

Like you ain't never knew my circumstance
Like I ain't never told you from the get advanced
I swear this stress is about to make me go
and get my head examined
You know my girl
You know my struggle
You know my troubles

I'm falling in love and I know it G
Cause I ain't never had no girl do
what she's done for me
I feel like I'm married and I'm leaving my family,
but God damn,
I ain't never felt this happy G

You ever had a girl make you feel like you were a
kid again?

So, baby I promise we both gon' have fits again
I'ma hold your hand and have these fits again
Cause I ain't leaving you until we have kids one
day, and that's the last time I'll ever call you a
bitch again

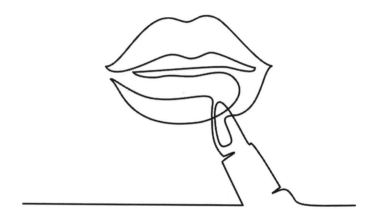

GLAD I GOT TO KISS YOU

I'm glad I got to kiss you,
but baby girl,
I miss you
I understand the timing is wrong but if you're
finding yourself please don't take too long

I'm your friend before anything
I'm just curious to know how life's treating you?
How's everything?

Lucky the guy that gives you a wedding ring,
because they don't make them like you anymore
So, I apologize in advanced for wanting more

I mean how can I not get curious when you're over
here crying for an idiot that didn't appreciate you
You don't know what you got until it's gone
So if you're finding yourself
please don't take too long

Just glad I got to kiss you
So, I wrote this for you to let you know that
I really do miss you

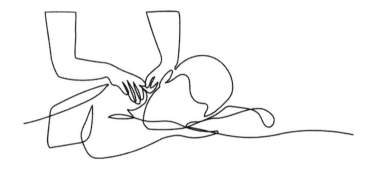

SOME OF US SAY FUCK IT

Some of us say fuck it, and find somebody else
Some of us say fuck it, I rather stay by myself
Some of us say fuck it and give up
on everyone else
Some of us say fuck it, there's nobody else

I'd rather stay with you and go through hell
Some of us say fuck it, I don't want nobody else
But sometimes you got to say fuck it,
and love yourself

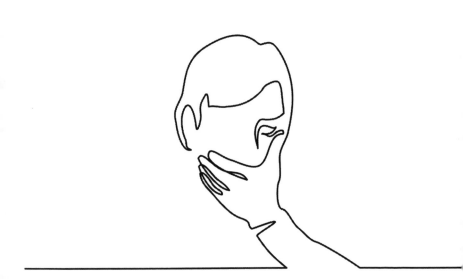

THE WORSE THAT I TREATED HER

The worse I treated her, the more she wanted me
to be with her
She caught me cheating
But I pleaded and admitted that I did it
So, she said if I would change
she would remain my main
So, I went along with the game
Promising I'd change
Cause why would I lose my main
for these hoes that I gained?
I pretended like things weren't going to be the
same
She believed me
She needed to believe me,
cause even though she knows
I'm a player, she does not want to leave me

Yea she needs me
She needs me for her happiness
In return, I give her crapiness'
And even though she met a good guy, he's no fun
She'd rather listen to the lies of the bad guy who
makes her cry; while seeking advice from the good
guy who is dying inside to hold her

I don't understand
I don't even touch her
I don't hold the door open for her
I don't get her gifts to express how much
I adore her

She's wifey
Why would I?
She's already infatuated with my deep lies and her
late cries to her friends asking, why?
Why am I with him?
Why do I love him?

Because the worst I treated her the more she
wanted me to be with her

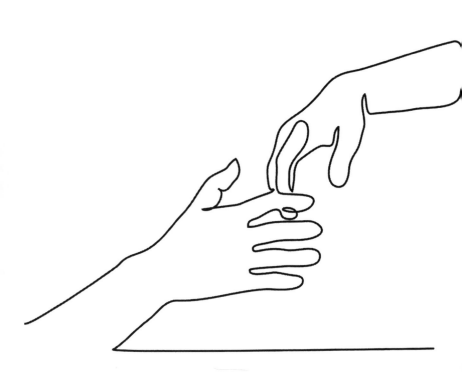

A LOVE UNSPOKEN

A love unspoken
Does she deserve a name?
I'd rather not share because in her,
I found love and pain
Am I selfish for not giving you a title?
When you're the alpha and omega
of a love I'll always idolize
You were my MVP
You were important
You were my first pick
You were my Michael Jordan

FIRST DATE JITTERS

First date jitters
Get off the phone
Look her in the eyes
Smile because she's gorgeous,
and she thinks your handsome
She asked about your art and then some
She wants ice cream
I give her ice cream
What a mess I am with this ice cream
She probably thinks I'm goofy with this ice cream
I need napkins on top of napkins
Talks about the past
I really don't want to talk right now,
but she's intriguing,
so I have to talk right now
She wants to walk right now
I don't do ice creams and walks right now
Yet I'm here walking and talking right now
I'm too quiet right now
Her thoughts are a riot right now
Cause the Most High is the highest right now
You have her up so high right now
How can she ever get that high right now?
I want to go with the flow right now
First date jitters
Get off the phone
Look her in her eyes
Smile because she's gorgeous,
and she thinks your handsome
Now give her a little piece of you and then some

I NEVER HAD A CHICK LIKE THIS

I never had a chick like this
Telling me my flaws like this
Analyzing me like this
Memorizing my poems like this
Giving me a back rub like this
How did I get so lucky like this?

All I wanted to do was smash this chick
I never had a chick like this
Nice lips
Nice tits
Nice hips
Nice mindset and shit

Asking about work and shit
Telling me I'm worth it all and shit
Telling me men like me rarely exist

Should I exit this?
Am I a fool for letting her go like this?
Am I going to be the reason for her to say men
ain't shit?
At least I told her how it is from the start and shit
But God, what did I do for you to send me a chick
like this?

You know I ain't built for this
Cause as soon as I wife her I'll lose all interest
I need to be alone like this
Someone to bone when I feel alone like this
She doesn't deserve for me to think like this
Act like this
Be dry like this
I hate when she asks me questions like this
I'm selfish like this

She wanted me to fuck her like this
But then got selfish like this
Now she wants me to love her like I'm it
But we'll never be shit

WHAT IF CONDOMS CAME WITH QUESTIONS?

What if condoms came with questions?
Do you love her?
Do you know her?
Will you protect her?

Would you still go inside her?
Would you take something from her you can never
give back?

What if condoms came with questions?
Would you question more what she means to you?
Would you tell her from the start that she isn't shit
but an open wrapper?
Do you love her?
Do you know her?
Will you protect her?

THE MOST HIGH

You were the most high
The most fly
I had you up there like the Most High
We came close
You and I
A series of almost but till then you'll remain
The most high
The most fly
We came close
You and I
A series of almost

WAS IT REAL?

What's real is the fact that every girl I've dated
since you has tasted your lips
Every girl I've dated since you has learned every
letter of your name
Not because I've told them but because it was
tattooed all over my heart
I've tried lying to them, but the truth you are to me
always reveals itself and the hesitation in my voice
makes my face crooked

What's real?
That when you aren't around, my body screams
"I love you," even when I'm holding hands with
another
That no matter what I did I couldn't control these
emotions that were trapped in my thoughts
The fact that I knew from the moment I laid eyes
on you that you would be mine
That even when you rejected my good intentions
I knew not how to forget you

All My Muses in One Room

I always reminded you how you'd end up with me,
and you did
How you would laugh at me, telling everyone I was
the only one in love
How in denial were you?
How in denial was I to believe you at times
Our story will forever be in denial of true
happiness until you allow love to love you
Until you allow yourself to love the love you're
afraid to lose
I won't call you a coward because I'm afraid too

But what's real?
That months after I got you I lost you?
Or that years after I've known I loved you one day
I'll say I loved you?

What's real?
I don't know
I can only feel
They say feelings fade like old photographs
So what's real?

THE WAY I SEE LOVE

I never stare at the image for too long
I feel as if I do it becomes a part of me
So, I look away looking as if I never looked at all
The way I see love

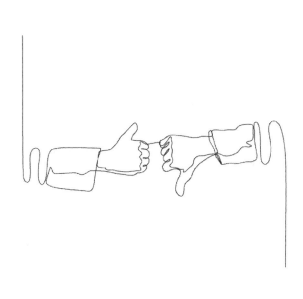

DON'T TELL ME YES, DON'T TELL ME NO

Don't tell me yes
Don't tell me no
Don't tell me stay
Don't tell me go
Don't tell me here
Don't tell me there
Don't teach me how
Don't show me now
Let me learn at my own pace
Let me live in this place
Don't take me to places that only exist in your
words
Cause words are only letters we express together

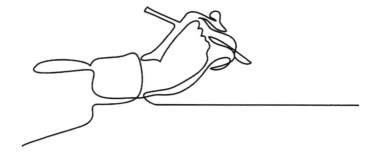

WHEN YOUR INK RUNS DRY

When your ink runs dry
It causes your pen to die
When your ink runs dry
The words have no life

WHAT DREAMS MAY COME

After I fought you for you,
I fought the demons inside of you
But still, you couldn't believe I'd stay for you
Those voices in your head convinced you it was too
good to be true
That only a mad man would endure the fires of hell
just to love you
Well, I'm no Robin Williams so this isn't What
Dreams May Come
But love will prove true so long as we find each
other in the next realm

BLACK

You wonder why I always wear black?
I wear black for the times you told me, "I was
afraid of the dark"
I wear black for the times you told me I wasn't
bright I wear black because I am my own light
I wear black to show you that I can make the
darkest color seem so white
So that when the sun hits me I can stand in its
shadow and still be me
I wear black for the dark thoughts you used to
share with me
I wear black to show you that no matter how much
darkness you throw at me, I'll always embrace your
negativity and in return bless you with positivity

FUCK SAYING THE RIGHT WORDS JUST TO FUCK YOU

Fuck saying the right words just to fuck you
I tried that and still lost you
All you ever wanted was a man to love you But
instead, I lusted you
You wanted a man that would spend his entire life
with you
Talks of kids and a family, how come I didn't find
the wife in you?
Seen too many hoes in this city
I guess I only see the trife in you

It must be this city, cause as soon as I turn good
for you you'll only reverse it all on me with no pity
Pretty, oh you're so pretty, and I've been alone for
way too long to not let your looks get up in me
See, you knew this would happen and how typical
You only care about yourself, so hypocritical
But everything happens for a reason and people
change like the seasons
I chose to not love you, and ended up playing
myself Because all I ever wanted was the good
between your legs

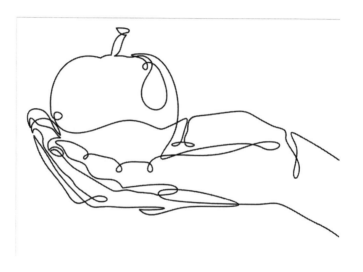

NAÏVE

She used to be so naïve for a ni**a
You know, that blind in love for a ni**a
Even when a ni**a would cheat

She used to take him back because that was her
ni**a
Till the day she started saying, "fuck a ni**a"
Then a good ni**a came along
But she couldn't tell the difference between a good
and a fuck ni**a
Now all her ni**as are gone so she feels all alone

CRAZY

What is love?
Man, love is that shit that makes you act crazy
Not crazy like you're going to kill somebody crazy,
but crazy like man, I feel crazy for somebody crazy

That type of crazy that if you were the type to be
lazy you'd no longer be lazy
Cause shit, you in love now so lazy isn't you
anymore

Crazy like the air smells different crazy and when
you look at the sky it isn't just blue it's that blue
inside of you crazy
That blue you feel when you ain't with her, crazy
Crazy like you would write her name on a sheet of
paper and one sheet of paper isn't enough to
express how crazy you feel about her, crazy

All My Muses in One Room

Shit so crazy that if a real crazy person were to talk
to you everything would make sense, crazy
Crazy like man, I am the definition of crazy but
that crazy in love crazy
Crazy like when she treats me like shit I'm crazy
enough to stick around crazy,
I know this might sound crazy, but lately you
haven't been acting like that once in love crazy
with my crazy

I have to be crazy to leave you
But I guess you aren't crazy about me anymore, so
I have to let you go
At least now I know how crazy love can make you
feel

HEAT OF THE MOMENT

Cause things are said in the heat of the moment
That's your girl, but you don't own it
You gotta make it worth it so she can enjoy it

We got options but I've been out too many nights
to know there are no options, baby
Cause at the end of it all, I still choose you, but
we're breaking up and we're making up, and all I
want is for you to know I'm not giving up no
matter what is said in the heat of the moment
Cause that's all it is
The heat of the moment

WET

I've never seen a girl so wet before
Wet like drenched in sweat
I've never felt it so wet, ever
So wet I can feel it dripping down my leg
Wet I tell you
So wet if we make love in the ocean,
the ocean would be jealous

WITHOUT HAVING TO TOUCH YOU

My poems are here to seduce you
Make you mad
Make you smile
Make you remember
Make you feel without having to touch you

IF PEOPLE WERE SEX

If people were sex, you'd be the first kiss
You'd be the clothes on the floor
If people were sex,
you'd be submissive but in bed only
If people were sex,
you'd be my favorite position
Doggy style
Hair pulling and smacks on the ass
If people were sex,
you'd be the ocean of wetness I drown in

If people were sex,
you'd be the open legs I walk into
You'd be the porno I've never made
You'd be the first personal video I've always
wanted to record but never had the courage to do
so
If people were sex,
you'd be the stare before the kiss
The anticipation before the excitement
If people were sex,
you'd be my favorite part

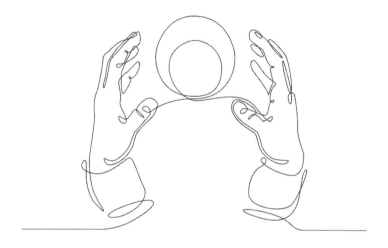

PUZZLE

You were my puzzle and who doesn't love puzzles?
I couldn't wait to piece you together
but instead at times I only broke you apart
just so I wouldn't have to let you go
You were my favorite, and at times it puzzles me
how you still are

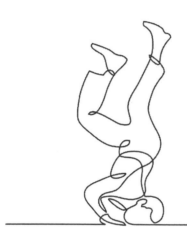

THESE THOUGHTS ABOUT YOU THAT I CAN'T GET OVER.

There's these thoughts about you that I just can't
get over, because I can only think about bending
you over I want to eat you
All of you leaving no leftover
I want to play hide and seek under these covers
I want to touch, lick and ache with passion like
we're secret lovers
I want to fuck but not love you
I want to give you something you can't get over

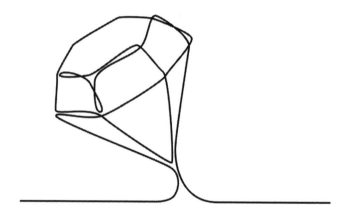

THE SECOND FIRST TIME I SAW HER

The second first time I saw her,
she was at the liquor store buying wine
Ironically enough,
it was valentine
How can I approach her?
She's a beauty
All I want to do is hold her
I said a few words but I can't remember what I told
her
She denied me then and denied me after I said fine,
we'll be friends
I'll make her fall in love with laughter, but the
more she laughed the more I fell for her
Cause if I couldn't make her mine, I was sure going
to try hard as hell

WRITERS BLOCK

Writers block,
so I pick up every block that's blocked a writer from
writing and make a pyramid
A pyramid of untold stories

YOU WILL NEVER BE THAT GIRL

You will never be that girl
The girl ni**as want to be with
You're just the girl ni**as want to be
in the sheets with
You're not the girl ni**as want to take to nice
places, spending money they can't afford, to eat
with
You will never be that girl
See, you open your legs so ni**as run inside you
You break down your walls so they come inside
you
Now you're naked still trying to hide
those insecurities
I mean, a girl like you has no purity
Nobody knows you call them baby
Nobody knows about those feelings you've been
dealing with lately
Wondering why you're not that girl
The one that makes him smile and not just cum
The one that he spends days dreaming about
That girl
Not the one he hides behind locked doors wrapped
up in bed sheets
You've offered him your time
He used it as a down payment to lay you away
in his bedroom
I don't mean to disrespect you, but see,
you don't even respect you,
and yet you want to be that girl?
The one he holds hands with in public?
No, you're just the one he fucks with
You want him to wife you
You want to be the one he talks about because he
really likes you, but you're not that girl
You will never be that girl

THE REASONS WHY I DID NOT WIFE YOU

There is a reason why I did not wife you
Not because I didn't like you, but because the guy
that I was didn't deserve to be with a girl like you
You know?
A creep
The one you text at 3 am
Pants on and shoes on my feet
95 miles on 95 just to beat
My mind on your body every time I want to eat
You deserve better
So, I let you go and let God guide you to the man
that will forever love you
The one that will ultimately wife you

I'VE BEEN BUSY (STUDYING YOUR BODY)

I've been busy
Busy studying your body as if there's an exam at the end of this
I've learned every birth mark, every curve, every part of you unseen by the light of day
See, I've been busy
So busy I've forgotten to make note of the parts I like the most
Memorization has become my best friend
Getting to know you has become my favorite routine
So, when people ask what happened to my writing, all I can say is I've been busy
Busy so busy thinking of the important words to describe you perfectly

KISSING HER

Kissing her is like catching a fresh breathe of air after holding it for so long.

I CAN FEEL THE OCEAN DRIPPING OUT OF HER

When I kiss her, I can feel the ocean
dripping out of her
I am harder than a rock about to do the rock
bottom on that pussy
I want to wrestle her into submission
See, she's the type that's not submissive, but when
we're in bed, she's the witness to how weak her
knees become when I'm inside of her
It's funny because our mouths are doing the same
things our bodies are
My tongue is exploring hers,
and hers is exploring mine

I can feel her breathing on me as if I've taken her
breath away
We aren't fucking
Man, I don't know what the fuck we are doing
I just know I've never been to this part of sex town
before cause I get lost in her curves
I get lost in her skin
I get lost in her eyes and in the way she looks at
me

When I go in deeper, the only three words she keeps
on saying to me is "I hate you" but see this isn't no
regular "I hate you"
This is the "I hate that I love you" I hate you
I hate that I like it that I hate you
See, hate is just as strong as love, but she can't admit
that she's loving it

She's forever in denial, but when she's in the mood
for me she knows exactly what numbers to dial
Cause I mean, there's a difference between fucking
and doing this love hate sex we are doing
I don't think we can even describe it
See, my only mission is to leave her satisfied and I
don't get mine until she gets hers
She's my priority and if she isn't coming then I am
not coming cause when I kiss her, I can feel the
ocean dripping out of her
But I just don't want to explore it
I want to own it

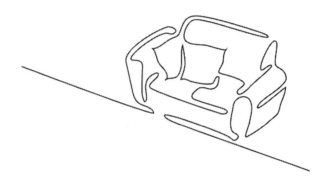

LOST WORDS

Stuck finding the right words
Funny thing is, I write words, but when it comes to
her, I can't find hers
So, I stay quiet hoping that my silence can be some
sort of sign language she can confide in
Cause the feelings I feel for her, I can't define them

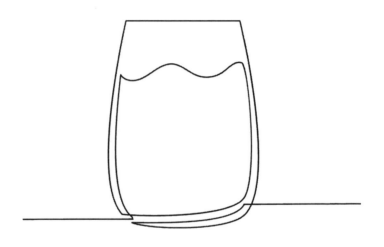

HER BODY LOOKED AS IF THE PERFECT ARCHITECT DESIGNED HER

Her body looked as if the perfect architect designed
it Her eyes carried the color of the sky as if the sun
was present
Her face was as if God came down from heaven and
designed it himself
She wasn't an angel, but she was close
Her lips must have been made by a fallen angel
because they spoke the softest sin
Her stare was the pure definition of the word
seduction
Her hair was a hurricane storming all over her
shoulders
Her heart was like the north pole but a bit colder

ONE-NIGHTSTAND

She said she is tired of one-night stands
So, she decided to sit this one down to get to know
my mentality
She said she felt attracted, she wanted me not my
sexuality
She said she wanted to fall in love with reality
She said she loves me but we can never be lovers
She said she thinks of me before her eyelids kiss
each other at night
She said her dreams are filled with fairytales
She said she loves me
She said that she's done lusting for me
She said she's done hunting for me
She asked when will I approach her?
Teach her about love, if I can coach?
If we can make this love our culture
She said she loves me like the moon misses the sun
Like the stars light up the skies at night
She said she loves me
She said when will I get the courage to approach
her? Love her, mold her, hold her like the diamond
ring
I carefully select before I own her
She said she loves me, but she doesn't want
another one-night stand

YOUR KISSES LEAD ME TO OTHER MISSES

Your kisses lead me to other misses
Now you will never know if I'll miss them
I gave you specific flowers and my pride was with them
I slowly gave you powers
Because not too many women take my minutes or my hours
Not too many women see the side of me that is not a coward

So, tell me why?
Why would you leave our garden?
Is it cause your heart became hardened?
Is it that you missed our cute behavior like we were in kindergarten?
We like each other but won't admit it
So, here's a flower so you'll never forget this love one day existed
We like each other but won't admit it

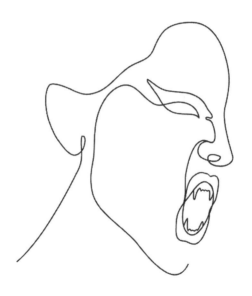

SHADOW

Her skin, darker than my shadow
Wherever I go, she will follow
She's always there quiet
Always present in my solitude
Greeting me with lots of emotions and gratitude
Sometimes she has attitude
Sometimes she confines herself inside her own
solitude
We talk without words, intimate expressions
We hide behind these walls, lost in affection
We kiss
We hug
No sexual intention
My shadow and I
A perfect combination

MARCH TOWARDS APRIL

March towards April
Maybe May might join June
So, you and I can get lost in July skipping August
and September
To not remember last October where you told me to
stay sober cause November got much colder
Where you cried on my shoulder, waiting for the
gifts of December
Where you said you wanted me forever
But January came and February came and your name
no longer taste the same when I speak of you

THAT LIQUOR BRINGS THE REAL OUT OF PEOPLE

That liquor brings the truth out of people
You get the whose and when out of people
That "I like you but never told you" sober out of people
The tears I could've never cried when I was with you out of people
You mean to tell me liquor brings the real out of people?
Brings the fear out of people?
That feel out of people?
That "I'm going to fuck you up" out of people
"cause now I'm brave" out of people?
Man, fuck people
I rather sip the truth in this liquor

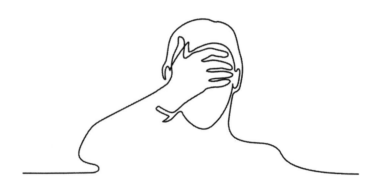

WAS IT REAL OR ALL IN MY HEAD?

Was it real or all in my head?
Was it real or was it all in my bed?
She said, 'do you remember what you said?"
Or was that the liquor whispering in your head?
No not the one with a brain, the other one instead

Now she's screaming
Now she's crying
Now she's all upset
I hate you
I hate men
I hate consequences that comes with being
interested "Was it real or was it all in my head?"
She said

WHY DO YOU ONLY LOVE ME
WHEN YOURE INTOXICATED?

Why do you only love me when you're intoxicated?
Didn't you listen when I told you that I hate it?
Cause you're calling me like you're missing me
But when you're back to being sober, you're just
dissing me
Can't you see this is why I distance me?
Don't you understand what distance means?
She's drunk off her ass and I know it G
But she's spilling her soul to me
She said listen, please listen closely
I ain't never let no man get this close to me
You cut me deep ni**a

You hurt me
I made mistakes but I ain't made them purposely
Do you love me?
Would you fuck me?
That's the liquor talking
I'm sorry
My friends got me drinking and all of that got me
thinking why are you not with me?

I replied, because I feel like you only
love me for the sex
Like when you're not sipping Jack or Henny I ain't
shit Why do you only love me when you're
intoxicated?
This is just a story about some drunk poetry and how
drunk she has to be to spill out her love for me

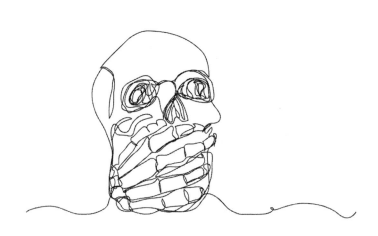

PICK YOUR POISON

Cause people are looking for love like it's hiring
Ain't that chasing tiring?
Pick your poison cause I'm looking for someone
that's inspiring
Someone who can mentally seduce me to the point I
no longer need to write these poems
Pick your poison
I want someone that can set a fire inside of me
A love so deep it will never get tired of me
If this is you, please apply here cause right now I'm
hiring

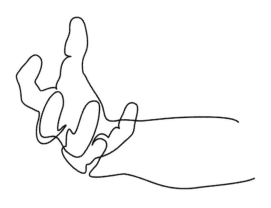

UNFAITHFULLY YOURS

"Unfaithfully yours"
Were the words I read when I opened your letter
Where you said we no longer should be together
You said you've reached a point of no return
To let it go and let it burn
I wasn't surprised
I already read it in your eyes
You expressed that you met another man
Said it all started as friends
How unfaithful you have been
How we should move on because of your selfish
sins
Now I stand here on my own looking at our home
Knowing that from here on, you are gone
I wish you well even though you've
put me through hell
I rather be alone than sit here forever trying to
dwell Unfaithfully yours

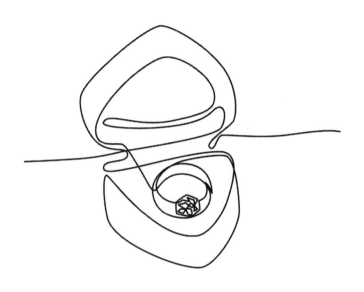

PRESALE

I wish I could have a drink with you
Sip liquor and tell you what I think of you
Your eyes, your hair, your lipstick
How are you?
How is life, how's it been for you?
Did you make it to that happy place?
Did you finish that unhappy race?
Do you still remember the talks after dark while
sitting in my car?
Talking about life on mars
The poison?
The poems?
Your exes and if I know them?
My exes and the late texts and how you would trust
me enough not to wear a latex, or the conversations
about our fake friends?
Our fights?
The bottles of jacks that would end up in play fights?
The love making?
The love hating?
The times you would recite my favorite lines from
liquor times that left my mind and heart aching?
Are you breaking?
Is this too much?
Too detailed?
Welcome to memory lane
This is your presale

BEFORE KISSING YOU ON PURPOSE

I can tell by your past you've been broken
Sometimes all it takes is a broken heart for us to
give up hoping
You have no one to go to, no one to cope with
No one to tell your troubles, outside of the late-
night shots you take by double
Sinking yourself in liquor doing things to yourself
to see what makes the pain go away quicker
So, you go on dates and you love hate these men
that wear capes thinking that you're a hoe and that
they need to save you, but they don't even know a
spec about you
So, they try to seduce you and firmly introduce you
to their friends pretending to like you
Hoping that by the end of the night you're tipsy
enough for him to fuck you
What an ugly world
The things we do for pink matter
Emotionally manipulating a woman just to have her
Not giving a fuck about the cause and effect, or
disaster you can leave in her life after
So, ask yourself, is it really worth it?
Just know that I rather get to know your mind before
kissing you on purpose

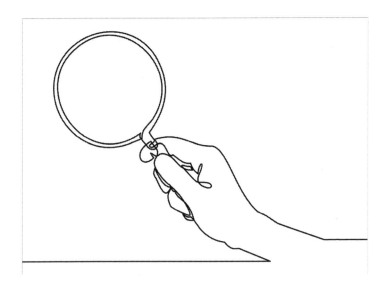

SOME LETTERS

See everything I've ever wanted this year I have
accomplished
I spoke to the universe and what it said left me
astonished
I wanted the letter "A" but "A" was too confused
My lust it didn't refuse and the letter "B" always
remained "B" because no matter what happens she's
still in love with me
The letter "C" no longer sees the good in me
So "D" got dicked down and now hates all of me
"E" became more of my escape but she's just my hoe
and I have no cape
"F" fucked me over but I am glad that it's over
Because I found "G" and "G" is nothing but good
and good is all I ever wanted, but now I got it all
figured out
Love is just a word put together by some letters
If it isn't you then it's her and maybe that's why we
will never be together
Keep your mental and emotions off the table
Love can only hurt you if you let her
Sincerely, some letters

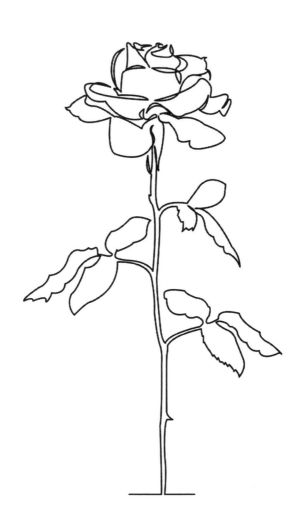

FLOWERS

We sat for hours talking about the stars, moon, and
flowers
I finally built the courage to walk up to her
To give her this flower
Because cowards do not give flowers and this flower
is ours
So, in this very moment we are infinite, no minutes,
no hours

LITTLE WHIP CREAM

She was the little whip cream of this dessert I was
dying to have
Dying to taste and no matter where I looked, I
couldn't find it
Till that one night on my dinner table she laid there
looking delicious and ready for me
So, I spread her over that forbidden fruit and sunk
my teeth in, licking her un wasted residue from my
lips
Maybe I sinned that night because the bitter sweet
taste it left in my mouth kept me from expressing
any emotion
It was exactly what I expected
I'm just glad I satisfied this craving that kept me
curious and at times, furious

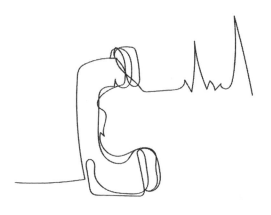

EXCHANGE NUMBERS

We exchange numbers
We fuck and then we forget each other's names
You change
I change, and the rest remains the same

MEN

We lie
We cheat
We're ready for the next who's ready for us to beat
How cold can we be?
Sexting Texting
Asking her to meet at 3 a.m. in the morning
My intentions are bleak
Cause all I want is her naked body next to me
As we pretend to make love, we reside in lust
My intentions are just to fuck
See, we don't care about your name
We don't care for romance
We just want a quickie
A little glance then on to the next one
This ain't shit to me
It's pure fun
While you're thinking I want more of you
The next moment I'm gone
Men, how cruel are we?
Walking around with no values
We lie
We cheat
I love you but I cheated
Please forgive me
We aren't meant to be

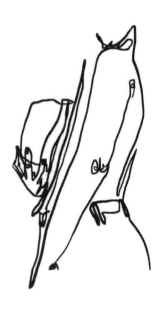

HELD BACK ON ME LIKE DETENTION

You've held back on me like detention
I still remember the first rejection when you asked
what were my intentions?
Not knowing you would fall
Fall into whatever you call this at all I clearly don't
know what this is
I just know it exists
Look how the tables have turned
From months of denying this fire that burns
You like me today but what about tomorrow?
You clearly don't know
You reject Cupid's arrows
You've been damaged by the events of your past
but how can we ever be if you do not let go of that
trash? I guess we will find out when we finally fall
If we ever fall at all

JUST A MEMORY

I'm a kisser
I would kiss her
So, we made love like no other
So, I can miss her
She said please remember me
Please take pictures
Now she's just a memory

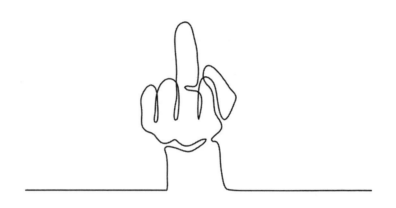

SIGN LANGUAGE

I guess the encounter of that kiss meant nothing
because our lips decided to meet
And communicate in sign language because the
words that it wanted to speak do not exist

AS CONFUSED AS SHE IS

If you ask me why I still care for her
I really don't know
I have asked myself that question about a million
time The only explanation I came up with is that I'm
intrigued by her mess
From the way she can't control her emotions
To the way she fights her sleep
From the way I can see her thinking and fighting her
own thoughts right in front of me
I don't know why I care
I just do
Maybe I'm as confused as she is

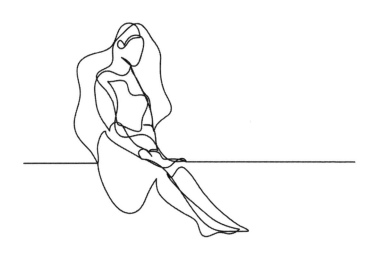

YESTERDAY

Yesterday was filled with anger and lots of desire
I'm a mixture of emotions and burning fire
It's a love hate thing that we both feel within
Filled with sins and memories that make this piece
of writing hard to begin
I can't even continue, these emotions got me stuck
in the rear view
To be continued...

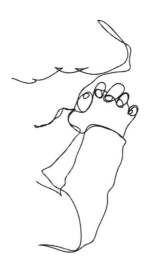

THE ACCIDENT

She got in an accident not too long ago
Scars on her neck, elbows, nose, hips, ribs nearly
alive
How did it come to this?
Would I live?
She repeated in her mind as she's rushed to the
hospital for life support
Thank God she wasn't too cool for the safety belt
You don't know life until death introduces itself
She's only 19
Only 19
Now imagine that phone call to her mother from the
accident scene
What a moment
What a moment
I wish I could fast forward
I cried so much it's like the clouds poured it

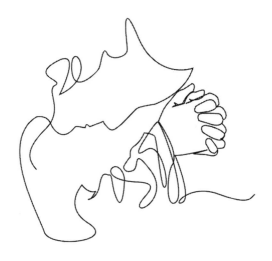

THE POISON THAT TORTURES ME

I need to do more than just drink
Do more than just think, because I got these
feelings inside of me that I just can't shrink
I guess it's my memories
I guess it's these injuries I acquired through the
poison that tortures me
There's no solution
There's no seclusion
I'm trapped in my thoughts
I'm trapped in illusions
I'm a walking confusion
I can't understand
I haven't met anyone who can
Are these words weak because they
come from a man?
Should I leave them unknown and hide it from
them?

DAD SAID

My dad said, "go ahead son. conquer the world"
My dad said, "strap up before fucking these girls"
My dad said, "always open the car door"
My dad said, "give her your coat when she's cold"
My dad said, "never kiss and tell. Sex stories
should never be told."
My dad said, "never use the same story. Shit tends
to get old"
My dad said, "never let the bullshit get to my head"

I wish my dad had said son you're a very good man,
instead
Wish dad said sorry we never caught up with
moments we never said
I wish dad said I'm proud of you cause you made it
all on your own and now you're all grown, moved
out from home, but this part of dad will forever be
unknown
My dad said, but this is what I wish my dad had
said instead

SEARCH

I'll find a girl exactly when I need to,
and if I haven't yet I know the day will come
when I will finally meet you
Please let me remind you I'm in no hurry,
because my hopes to find you have slowly been
buried
I wish my vison of you was clear but love needs
glasses because I only see blurry as more time passes
What a shame
What a shame
Will I ever know your name?
Will I ever hold your hand?
Will we ever be together at the end or is this just a
journey?
Is it that I look for you poorly?
I wish I knew, but I don't
I'm lost in the thoughts of you
I'm lost and it's all because of you
I guess I'll find out when I finally meet you

PRETTY GIRL

Mama always said, "treat these women the same way
you want your sister to be treated"
So, I asked my sister and she said she always cheated
Never on some hoe shit
I'm sure she had her reasons
I'm sure it was because she was constantly
mistreated, but she found the right dude so her
mission was completed
Her advice always kept me undefeated but I'm tired
of the games
I'm tired of these women who love to complain,
cause attention is what they love to attain and whose
sweet dreams is to kiss in the rain and hear things
only lovers can explain
Pretty girl
Pretty girl
I wonder, where are you?
If you're close or if you're far, how long should I
wait?
Would I ever take you on a date?
I just hope you find me before it's too late

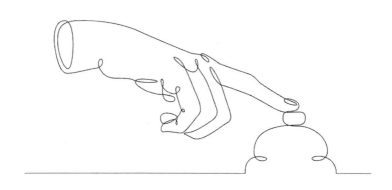

TODAY I CONFESS

Today I confess that all my life I haven't tried to
be the best
Today I confess that at times I am sensitive and
maybe more than the rest
Today I confess that I have a lot of things bottled
inside of my chest
The reality of life has all of my thoughts
suppressed Sometimes I wish I had a rewind button
or even a reset
Sometimes I find myself drinking more than the
rest Sometimes I don't remember anything, nor
forget
I'm frozen in time finding myself so I can keep
moving forward to achieve what's meant to be
mine
A few confessions

IT WASN'T VALENTINE

I brought you flowers and it wasn't even
Valentine's, but if you ask me this is rare in a man
to do from time to time
I held your hands and kissed your lips and you
weren't even mine
We fought, we argued, but the obstacles I didn't
mind
I just wanted to let you know that it doesn't have
to be Valentine's for you to feel like you're mine

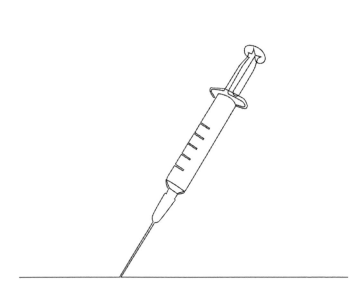

MEET AGAIN

She said we have a deal to meet again, but this would
be goodbye because I will never see her again
I took the offer and since then I've never seen her
again
Seems like the deal was to never see us again
I think she just wanted to see what that meeting
would feel like if we could be us again

MAKE UP SEX

She recited my poems after sex
She knew every word by heart
I was impressed
Then she got dressed
We used to get drunk just to tell the truth
Make up sex is all we used to do

IF WORDS COULD KILL

I wish I could kill you with my words
Cut you deep like a sword with my words
Take your breath away then give it back with my
words
Wish you could feel me with my words
Bring you closer with my words
So that I can whisper into your ear all these words
Make the hair on the back of your neck shiver with
my words
Make the butterflies in your stomach dance with
my words
Make your soul come out of your body with my
words
I want you to learn every letter to my words
The truth is, you are the inspiration for these
words Woman, I want to be your last and your first
I want to do things to you he can never do
Erase all the things any man has put you through
Give you a new memory
Take you to a spot you thought you could never be
Cause for you, I would move the stars, moon and
the galaxy
I would bring down angels from heaven and let
them sing to you a melody
Woman you are my Mona Lisa and I am your
Leonardo Da Vinci
Mixed with some Shakespeare, and there's no arrow
or spear cupid can aim here to make you fall this
deep
I never thought love can make you feel so strong,
yet so weak
I just want you here with me
If words could kill, this is how I truly feel

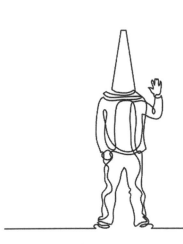

WHISPERS IN YOUR EAR

Can I whisper in your ear?
Can I tell you all the things that you want to hear?
Can you picture just you and I here?
Can I make all of your clothes disappear?
Are we not alone?
Baby I want to touch all bases until I make it home
You're my favorite girl, so can I seduce you?
Can I lick your neck?
I want to bite you softly but fuck you hard, no
disrespect
Damn you're so sexy
I get nervous when your next to me
You and I, baby that's ecstasy
Can I start by gripping your ass then slowly move
my hands to your chest?
Do I have to ask?
That look in your eyes screams out you won't regret
me
Now open your legs and let me

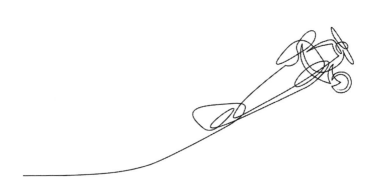

A TOY STORY

You wanted me like a child that just saw toy story
for the first time and begged mom for a Buzz
Lightyear toy
"To infinity and beyond," you said
You played with me like an action figure
Told me what I needed to hear so I could fly
And become what you needed me to be
Created this whole universe of fantasies that
brought me to life
I was no longer an action figure
It was real
I became something to the figment of your
imagination
Only to be left in the dust

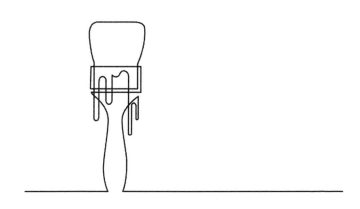

ALONE

Damn, I need to be alone for a little
I won't take long, it'll be just a little
I need me time at least for a little
I can't give you more of me because I only got this
little
Bear with me, I'm coping with this little
I'm hoping that you understand me a little
I got a lot of friends but only trust a little
I made this bubble and in it is me in the middle
I'm in my own world can I live for a little?
Cause lately all I do is give for a little
I want more than a little
I aspire to be more than a little
I'm sorry I won't take long, just a little
Block everything for a little
Get lost for a little
I promise I'll be back, it'll be just a little

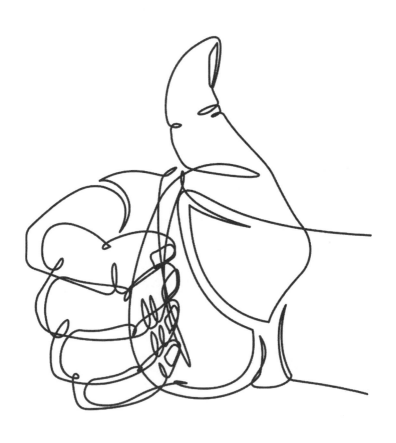

UGLY

I got nightmares I still wake up to
I got dreams I still sleep on
I got ugly things inside of me
Things I want to throw up
Disappointments in others, like when your father
said he'll show up but you waited till you fell asleep
cause he never did
How can you feel whole, when you're so incomplete?
Everything I want or need is inside of me
So, when I hurt others, I'm only hurting me

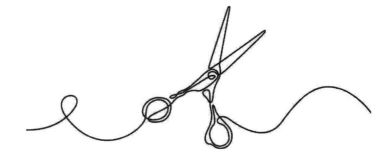

UNGIVING

Cause who would buy a birthday card and not give
it?
Who would ask for life and not live it?
Who would take, take, take, so ungiving
Cause you got me a cake with no candles
A bike with no handles
So incomplete, just like you, just like me

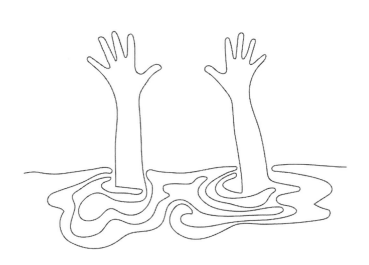

I WROTE ABOUT YOU IN PENCIL

I wrote about you in pencil because I didn't know
if ink was well worth it for you
I guess I had a feeling I'd come back
and have to erase you
Erase these words once written
The ink would've been too real
Too permanent and I couldn't take that risk on you
At least not anymore

GROWTH

Growing is painful
Any type of growth is painful
Spiritual growth
Physical growth
Mental growth
Financial growth
It's all painful
That's why people choose to not grow
When you start to walk as a child you fall,
it is painful
You get back up and try again
You want to grow financially
You have to save money
You want to grow physically
You have to lift weights
You want to grow mentally
You have to go through tough times
You want to grow spiritually
You have to sacrifice
Sacrifices are painful
You have to say no
When everyone says yes
You have to take a different path
When others take the same
Growing is painful
So, some people would rather choose
comfort over growth
You have to take the road less traveled
You either grow or stay the same

THIS IS FOR THE POETS

This is for the poets
The ones that know it
The ones that reopen scabs of pain
Just to give you a piece of them
Do you know what it takes
to write down a memory of pain?
To please the addicts that relate to your story?
The ones that feel the pain but do not know how
to express them?
The ones that are muted but desire to say
everything they can't express through words?
Do you know what is like to be
a giver of small stories?

Do you know what it feels like to reopen the pain?
To go back in time and feel exactly how you felt
just one more time
For the sake of this piece
I give you my pieces
I come in pieces
I am still whole
I am still complete but break myself for the
satisfaction of letting you know you are not alone
You are not muted
I speak for those that want to say so much,
but cannot

Meet the Author

Ronald Acevedo was born in Managua, Nicaragua before migrating to the US at the age of eight months old. Ronald attended a local Miami College before deciding to drop out and pursue his writing dreams. At the age of 11, Ronald started writing down song lyrics that soon evolved into poems. At the age of 22 Ronald wrote his first complete spoken word poem entitled Liquor Times. At which point, he started performing at local open mic events throughout Miami. At age 26 he felt inspired to write his first book, leaving all his muses in one room.

57054839R00124

Made in the USA
Columbia, SC
04 May 2019